Delicious Italian Beef

Ingredients:

- 750g pound beef brisket

- 2 onions (thinly sliced into rings)

- 2 tbsp corn starch

- Water (desired preference)

- 70g chili sauce

- 1 bay leaf

- 1 bunch of dried thyme (crushed)

- 1 garlic clove (minced)

- 10 Italian Bread Rolls

Method:

1.Start by trimming off any excess fat from the beef. Place it in a 6 quart/6 liter slow cooker along with onions and bay leaf.

2.In a mixing bowl, mix the chili sauce with thyme, salt, pepper and garlic. Combine well and pour it over the meat.

3.Cover the cooker and cook on low heat for approximately 10-12 hours.

4.Once the beef is cooked, transfer it along with the onions onto a serving platter and cover it with a foil.

5.Next, in a medium sauce pan, pour the remaining mixture and stir it together with cornstarch and water. Cook the mixture for approximately 2 to 3 minutes or until the gravy thickens.

6.Serve the beef on the Italian rolls and top it off with the gravy.

Nutritional Information:

Calories; 325, Fats 8g, Carbohydrates 35g, Protein 25g

Spinach and Mushroom Quiche

Ingredients:

- Disposable liner and non stick cooking spray

- 1 package frozen chopped spinach; thawed and drained

- 4 slices bacon

- 1 tablespoon olive oil

- 150g Portobello mushrooms; coarsely chopped

- 90g sweet red pepper; chopped

- 150g grated Swiss cheese

- 8 eggs

- 500ml whole milk or half and half

- 2 tablespoons fresh chives; snipped

- ½ teaspoon salt

- ½ teaspoon black pepper

- 60g cup biscuit mix

Method:

1.Line the slow cooker and spray liner with non stick spray.

2.Cook bacon until crisp; drain and crumble.

3.Heat olive oil and add mushrooms and pepper. Cook until tender then add spinach and cheese.

4.Combine eggs, milk, chives, salt, and pepper and stir into spinach mixture. Add the biscuit mixture and gently fold. Pour into slow cooker and sprinkle with prepared bacon crumbs.

5.Cook in slow cooker on low for 4 to 5 hours. If using high heat cook for 2 to 2.5 hours. Cool 15 to 30 minutes before serving.

Nutritional Information:

Calories; 431, Fats 31g, Carbohydrates 66g, Protein 25g, Sugar 2g

Chile Lasagna

Ingredients:

- 500g bulk breakfast sausage

- 130g chopped sweet green pepper; finely chopped

- 1 jalapeno pepper; stemmed, seeded, and finely chopped

- 5 eggs beaten lightly

- 2 teaspoons vegetable oil

- ½ a bunch of green onions; sliced

- ¼ snipped cilantro or parsley

- ½ teaspoon salt

- ½ teaspoon cumin

- 9 corn tortillas; 6 inch/15cm

- 200g Monterey jack cheese/hard cheese; shredded

- 1x 500g ounce jar green salsa

Method:

1.Lightly coat the inside of the slow cooker with non stick cooking spray.

2.Brown sausage in skillet and drain off fat. Add the sweet pepper and jalapeno pepper to skillet and cook over medium heat for 1 minute. Transfer sausage and peppers to bowl.

3.In the same pan cook eggs in hot oil just until set; stir to break up eggs. Combine eggs with sausage and peppers. Stir in green onions, cilantro, salt, and cumin.

4.Place 3 of the tortillas in the bottom of the slow cooker; it is fine if they over lap. Put half the egg and sausage mixture in the slow cooker and sprinkle with 1/4 of the cheese. Pour 2/3 of the salsa over the mixture in slow cooker. Continue layering until all tortillas, sausage mixture, and salsa are in slow cooker.

5.Cover and set to low heat for 3 to 4 hours. Let stand for 15 minute before serving. Can top with sour cream and cilantro if desired.

Nutritional Information:

Calories; 429, Fats 29g, Carbohydrates 18g, Protein 21g, Sugar 3g

Eggplant Sauce

Ingredients:

- 1 eggplant

- 2x 210g. cans diced tomatoes

- 180g. tomato paste (canned)

- 1x 120g. can sliced mushrooms; drained

- 60ml red wine (optional)

- 60ml water

- 75g onion (chopped)

- 2 cloves of garlic (chopped)

- 1 ½ teaspoon oregano

- 60g cup olives (pitted)

- 2 tablespoons fresh parsley; chopped

- Black pepper

- Parmesan cheese (shredded; optional)

Method:

1.Peel eggplant and cut into small cubes.

2.In the slow cooker combine the eggplant, onion, canned tomatoes with juice, tomato paste, mushrooms, wine, water, garlic, and oregano.

3.Cover the slow cooker and allow it to cook on low heat for approximately 7 to 8 hours.

4.Add the olives and parsley.

6.Serve over cooked noodles and sprinkle with Parmesan cheese.

Nutritional Information:

Calories; 346, Fats 4g, Carbohydrates 65g, Protein 13g, Sugar 5g

Tacos with Beef and Radish

Ingredients:

- 1,5kg beef; trimmed and cut into 2 inch/5cm cubes

- 1 large onion; sliced thin

- 4 chopped cloves of garlic

- 1 to 3 tablespoons chopped chipotle; canned in adobo sauce

- 1 teaspoon oregano

- 2 bay leaves

- Kosher salt

- 400g cabbage; thinly sliced

- 4 radishes (halved and thinly sliced)

- 15g fresh cilantro

- 2 tablespoons lime juice

- Corn tortillas

- Toppings: sour cream, salsa, jalapenos, shredded cheese

Method:

1.In the slow cooker toss together the beef, garlic, onion, chipotles, oregano, bay leaves, and salt. (tip: add just a bit of water to bottom to avoid sticking)

2.Cook on high for 3.5 to 4 hour or on low for 7 to 8 hours.

3.Twenty minutes before meat mixture is done wrap tortillas in foil and place in oven (350°F/180°C) for 5 to ten minutes to warm.

4.While tortillas are warming and meat is finishing up, toss together the cabbage, radishes, lime juice, and ¼ teaspoon salt.

5.Transfer the meat to a bowl and shred with a fork; save the broth. Strain the liquid into the meat and stir to combine.

6.Fill tortillas with beef and slaw; top with your choice of toppings.

Nutritional Information:

Calories; 521, Fats 6g, Carbohydrates 34g, Protein 57g, Sugar 5g

Chili Slow Cooker Style

Ingredients:

- 500g ground pork

- 500g pork shoulder; trimmed and cut into ½ inch cubes

- 300g bell pepper; chopped

- 450g chopped onion

- 3 minced cloves of garlic

- 3 tablespoons tomato paste

- 3 tablespoons chili powder

- 1 tablespoon cumin

- 2 teaspoons oregano

- ¾ teaspoon black pepper

- 6 tomatillos (quartered)

- 2 bay leaves

- 2x 450g cans plum tomatoes; chopped and drained

- 1 420g can pinto beans drained; no salt added

- 1 220g. can Mexican style tomato sauce

- 1 smoked ham hock

- 25g cilantro; chopped finely

- Bunch of green onion; chopped finely

- 110g crumbled queso fresco/cream cheese

- 8 lime wedges

Method:

1.Brown pork in skillet and transfer to slow cooker after draining fat.

2.Brown pork should pieces in skillet until browned and transfer to slow cooker after draining fat.

3.In skill sprayed with non stick spray sauté onion and pepper for 8 minutes; stirring often. Add garlic and sauté 1 minute more. Add tomato paste and cook for 1 minute; stirring constantly. Add onion mixture to slow cooker with meat.

4.Add chili powder, cumin, pepper, tomatillos, bay leaves, plum tomatoes, beans, tomato sauce, and ham hock. Cover and set slow cooker on high for 5 hours.

5.Remove bay leaves and ham hock; discard.

6.Ladle into serving cups or bowls; top with 1 tablespoon cilantro, cheese, green onions, and serve with a lime wedge.

Nutritional Information:

Calories; 357, Fats 14.4g, Carbohydrates 26g, Protein 27.7g

Chicken Enchilada

Ingredients:

- 1 teaspoon canola oil

- 150g onion; chopped

- 90g poblano/chili pepper, seeded and chopped

- 2 minced cloves garlic

- 1 ½ teaspoon chipotle chili powder

- 1x 420g diced tomatoes; drained and no salt added

- 1x 240g canned tomato sauce; Italian seasoned

- Cooking spray

- 300g rotisserie chicken breast; shredded

- 180g; white and yellow corn

- 1x 450g. can black beans; drained and rinsed

- 5 corn and flour tortillas

- 240g. shredded cheddar cheese; reduced fat

- Cilantro sprigs

Method:

1.1.Using a nonstick skillet heat on medium and add oil. Add onion, pepper, and garlic; cook until tender; about 6 minutes.

2.Stir in chili powder, tomatoes, and tomato sauce. Put half the tomato mixture in a blender. Remove lid of blender and let steam escape. Place a towel over blender and blend until almost smooth and pour into a bowl. Repeat process with the other half of tomato mixture.

3.Spray slow cooker with non stick cooking spray. Spread 3 tablespoons of tomato mixture on bottom of slow cooker. Mix the remainder of tomato mixture with chicken, corn, and beans.

4.Place one tortilla on the tomato mixture in slow cooker. Cover with half of the chicken mixture. Sprinkle with cheese; about 100g. Top with another tortilla and repeat process until all tortillas and chicken mixture are in slow cooker.

5.Cook on low setting for 2 hours or until the cheese is melted and the edges are browned.

Nutritional Information:

Calories; 295, Fats 10.3g, Carbohydrates 16g, Protein 24g

Sausage with Rice

Ingredients:

- 300g onions; chopped

- 100g; chopped

- 250ml water

- ½ teaspoon Cajun season

- ½ teaspoon thyme dried

- 500g skinless chicken (breast or thighs) cut into 1" cubes

- 240g sausage sliced

- 900g cooked rice

- 1x 420g canned tomatoes (diced with green chilies) undrained

- 500g medium size shrimp; peeled and deveined

- 900g cooked rice (garnish)

Method:

1. Combine the first 8 ingredients in slow cooker; cover and cook on low for 6 hours.

2. Stir in shrimp and cook 10 minutes longer on low or until shrimp is done.

3. Serve over hot cooked rice and garnish with chopped green onion if desired.

Nutritional Information:

Calories; 310, Fats 8.5g, Carbohydrates 14g, Protein 30g

Cabbage Rolls

Ingredients:

- 12 large cabbage leaves

- 450g onion; chopped

- 100g instant rice; uncooked

- 250g ground pork; lean

- 250g pork breakfast sausage; 50% lean

- ¼ teaspoon black pepper

- 1x 420g. can sauerkraut; shredded; drained and rinsed

- ½ teaspoon caraway seeds

- 400ml tomato juice; low sodium

- 2 tablespoon brown sugar light (optional)

- 3 tablespoons tomato paste

Method:

1.Cook cabbage leaves in boiling water until tender; about 3 to 4 minutes.

2.Sauté onion in skillet for 5 to 7 minutes or until tender; add rice stir and let stand for 15 minutes.

3.Combine rice, pork, and pepper. Fill cabbage leaf with a bit of the meat mixture and turn sides in and roll. Repeat for all cabbage leaves.

4.Mix caraway seed with sauerkraut. Put half the sauerkraut mixture into bottom of slow cooker after coating with non stick spray. Top layer of sauerkraut with half the cabbage rolls. Repeat this step with remaining sauerkraut and cabbage rolls.

5.Combine tomato juice, brown sugar, and tomato paste with a whisk. Pour tomato juice mixture over sauerkraut and cabbage rolls. Cook on low setting for 6 hours and serve.

Nutritional Information:

Calories; 287, Fats 10.8g, Carbohydrates 12.3g, Protein 17.7g

Sweet and Sour Chicken

Ingredients:

- 150g onion; chopped

- 75g sugar

- 80ml ketchup

- 100ml orange juice

- 3 tablespoons cider vinegar

- 2 tablespoons soy sauce; low sodium

- 1 tablespoon grated fresh ginger

- 1 pound skinless chicken (cubed)

- 500g pineapple chunks

- 1 bell pepper; large, cut into ¾ inch/2cm pieces

- 1 red pepper; large cut into ¾ inch/2cm pieces

- 600g cooked brown rice

Method:

1.Combine the first 12 ingredients in a slow cooker.

2. Cook on high for 4 hours or 6 hours on low covered.

3.Serve over hot brown rice.

Nutritional Information:

Calories; 332, Fats 3.4g, Carbohydrates 7.1g, Protein 18.4g

Roast Turkey

Ingredients:

- 300g onion; chopped

- 70g pitted olives

- 100g Julienne-cut and drained oil packed tomato halves sun dried

- 2 tablespoons lemon juice

- 1 ½ teaspoon garlic minced

- 1 teaspoon Greek seasoning mix

- ½ teaspoon salt

- ¼ teaspoon pepper

- 1 trimmed turkey breast (4 pounds)

- 130ml fat free chicken brother; low sodium

- 3 tablespoons all purpose flour

- Thyme sprigs

Method:

1. Put first 9 ingredients in slow cooker. Add 65ml chicken broth, cover and cook for 7 hours on low.

2. Whisk the remaining flour and chicken broth and pour into slow cooker. Cook for an additional 30 minutes on low setting.

Nutritional Information:

Calories; 314, Fats 4.9g, Carbohydrates 16.2g, Protein 57g

Fine Potato Soup

Ingredients:

- 3 slices bacon

- 150g onion; chopped

- 1,5kg potatoes; peeled and cut into slices

- 120ml water

- 500ml chicken broth; low sodium and reduced fat

- ½ teaspoon salt

- ½ teaspoon black pepper

- 400ml low fat milk

- 150g reduced fat cheddar cheese; shredded

- 120g sour cream (light)

- 4 teaspoons chopped chives

Method:

1. Cook bacon in skillet until crisp. Remove bacon from pan and add onion to drippings. Sauté for 3 minutes.

2. Put potato slices and onion in slow cooker after coating with non stick spray. Combine water with the next three ingredients and add to slow cooker. Cover and cook on low heat for 8 hours or until potatoes are tender.

3. Mash mixture with a potato masher. Stir in milk and cheese. Turn heat to high and cook for 20 minutes.

4. Serve in bowls topped with sour cream, chive, and crumbled bacon.

Nutritional Information:

Calories; 259, Fats 6.4g, Carbohydrates 9g, Protein 13.2g

Delicious Veggy Chili

Ingredients:

- 420g can of firm tofu (drained and cubed)
- 450g canned black beans (drained)
- 450g canned tomatoes (crushed)
- 4 onions (chopped)
- 2 red bell peppers (seeded and chopped)
- 2 green bell peppers (seeded and chopped)
- 4 cloves of garlic
- 2 tsp ground cumin
- ½ tsp ground black pepper
- 6 tbsp chili powder
- 2 tbsp dried oregano
- 2 tsp salt
- 2 tbsp white vinegar (distilled)
- 1 tbsp hot pepper sauce
- 120ml olive oil (extra virgin)

Method:

1.In a large skillet, heat the oil over medium heat.

2.Add the onions to it and cook until softened. Next add in the peppers, tofu and garlic and cook for approximately for ten minutes or until the vegetables start to turn brown and tender.

3.Now cook the beans in a slow cooker over low heat. Stir in all the vegetables and tomatoes and season it.

4.Cover and cook for approximately six to eight hours.

Nutritional Information:

Calories; 445, Fats 18.2g, Carbohydrates 58.2g, Protein 21.2g

Slow Cooker Spinach Sauce

Ingredients:

- 840g canned tomatoes (peeled and crushed)

- 300g frozen spinach (chopped, thawed and drained)

- 1 onion (chopped)

- 30g cup carrot (grated)

- 2 ½ tbsp red pepper (crushed)

- 5 garlic cloves (minced)

- 180g canned tomato paste

- 150g canned mushrooms (sliced and drained)

- 2 tbsp dried oregano

- 2 tsp salt

- 2 tbsp dried basil

- 2 bay leaves

- 60ml olive oil (extra virgin)

Method:

1.Combine olive oil with spinach, onion, garlic, carrots, tomato paste and mushrooms in a 5 quart/5liter slow cooker.

2.Add in the salt, pepper, oregano, bay leaves and tomatoes.

3.Cover and cook for approximately 4 hours over high heat. After 4 hours are up, stir and reduce the heat to low and cook for an additional 2 hours.

Nutritional Information:

Calories; 176, Fats 8.2g, Carbohydrates 25.1g, Protein 6.6g

Vegetarian Minestrone

Ingredients:

- 1,5liter vegetable broth

- 450g canned kidney beans (drained)

- 840g canned tomatoes (crushed)

- 900g spinach (freshly chopped)

- 1 onion (chopped)

- 2 large carrots (diced)

- 2 celery ribs (diced)

- 1 zucchini

- 150g green beans

- 1 tbsp parsley (minced)

- 3 garlic cloves (minced)

- ¾ tsp thyme (dried)

- 1 ½ tsp oregano (dried)

- 1 tsp salt

- 1/3 tsp ground black pepper

- 50g elbow macaroni (cooked)

- 25g Parmesan cheese (finely grated)

Method:

1.In a 6 quart/6liter slow cooker, combine the vegetable broth with kidney beans, green beans, tomatoes, onion, zucchini, celery and carrot.

2.Season it with garlic, thyme, parsley, oregano, salt and black pepper.

3.Cook the minestrone on low heat for approximately 7 to 8 hours.

4.Next, stir the spinach and macaroni into the minestrone and allow it to cook for another 15 minutes or so.

5.Top it off with grated Parmesan cheese.

Nutritional Information:

Calories; 138, Fats 1.7g, Carbohydrates 25.2g, Protein 6.9g

Slow Cooker Cassoulet

Ingredients:

- 500g navy beans (dry; soaked overnight)

- 1l mushroom broth

- 1 cube vegetable bouillon

- 1 onion

- 2 carrots (peeled and diced)

- 1 potato (peeled and cubed)

- 4 sprigs of parsley

- 1 sprig of rosemary

- 1 sprig of lemon thyme (chopped)

- 1 sprig of savory

- 1 bay leaf

- 2 tbsp olive oil (extra virgin)

Method:

1.In a large skillet, heat the oil over medium heat. Stir in the onion and the carrots and cook until it becomes tender.

2.In a slow cooker, combine the beans with the broth, bouillon, carrots, onion and bay leaf. Add in 100ml of water if required.

3.Season the mixture with parsley, thyme, rosemary and savory and allow it to cook on low heat for approximately 8 hours or so.

4.Next, stir in the potato and continue to cook for another hour.

5.Remove all the herbs and serve!

Nutritional Information:

Calories; 279, Fats 4.4g, Carbohydrates 47.2g, Protein 15.3g

Risotto with Fennel and Cheese

Ingredients:

- 2 teaspoons of fennel seeds

- 1 fennel bulb, cored and diced

- 200g of brown rice

- 1 carrot, chopped

- 1 shallot, chopped

- 2 cloves of garlic, minced

- 1l of chicken broth

- 400ml of water

- 80ml of dry white wine(optional)

- 360g of green beans

- 50g of shredded parmesan cheese

- 50g of pitted black olives, chopped

- 1 tablespoon of grated lemon zest

- ½ teaspoon of salt

- ½ teaspoon of pepper

Method:

1.Chop the carrot, the shallot, the black olives and core and chop the fennel bulb

2.Grate the lemon zest and mince the garlic

3.Place all of the ingredients into the slow cooker and stir until well mixed

4.Cook for three and a half hours on low

5.Stir and cook until desired heat is cooked all the way through

6.Serve and enjoy, try some parmesan cheese on top

Nutritional Information:

Calories: 242 kcal, Fats: 6 grams, Carbohydrates: 36 grams, Protein: 10 grams

Slow cooked beans

Ingredients:

- 450g of dried beans, mix pinto beans with black beans and kidney beans

- 1 onion, chopped

- 4 cloves of garlic, minced

- 1 teaspoon of thyme

- 1 bay leaf

- 1200ml of boiling water

- ½ teaspoon of salt

Method:

1.Place the beans in a large pot with the water, bring to a boil on high heat and cook for about one hour

2.Drain the beans

3.Chop the onion and mince the garlic

4.Add to the beans and stir well

5.Lower heat and cook for about three more hours

6.Add the salt and cook for 15 more minutes

7.Serve and enjoy

Nutritional Information:

Calories: 260 kcal, Fats: 1 gram, Carbohydrates: 48 grams, Protein: 15 grams

Black Bean with Mushroom Chili

Ingredients:

- 500g of black beans

- 1 tablespoon of extra virgin olive oil

- 30g of mustard seeds

- 2 tablespoons of chili powder

- 1 ½ teaspoons of cumin

- ½ teaspoon of cardamom

- 2 onions, chopped

- 500g of mushrooms, chopped

- 240g of tomatillos, husk them and rinse and chop

- 60ml of water

- 1300ml of mushroom broth

- 1x 180g can of tomato paste

- 2 tablespoons of minced garlic

- 120g of pepper jack cheese/hard cheese

- 110g of sour cream

- 25g of cilantro

- 2 limes cut into wedges

Method:

1.Place the beans in a large pot with water and boil on medium to high heat for about an hour

2.Drain and mix in the rest of the ingredients in a Dutch oven

3.Cook on low to medium heat for about five hours

4.Serve and enjoy, try with some sour cream and shredded cheese

Nutritional Information:

Calories: 306 kcal, Fats: 10 grams, Carbohydrates: 40 grams, Protein: 18 grams

Chickpea and Lentil Stew

Ingredients:

- 150g of chickpeas

- 1300g of squash, peeled and cut into chunks

- 2 carrots, peeled and sliced

- 1 onion, chopped

- 1 cup of red lentils

- 1liter of vegetable broth

- 2 tablespoons of tomato paste

- 1 tablespoon of ginger, minced

- 1 ½ teaspoons of cumin

- 1 teaspoon of salt

- ¼ teaspoon of saffron

- ¼ teaspoon of pepper

- 60ml of lime juice

- 70g of peanuts, chopped

- 15g of cilantro

Method:

1.Place the beans in a large crock pot and bring to a boil, cook for about an hour

2.Drain and combine everything but the peanuts and the cilantro in the slow cooker

3.Cook on low for about five hours

4.Serve and enjoy, sprinkle with cilantro and peanuts

Nutritional Information:

Calories: 294 kcal, Fats: 7 grams, Carbohydrates: 48 grams, Protein: 14 grams

Chickpea and Eggplant Stew

Ingredients:

- 75g of mushrooms
- 750ml of water
- 2 eggplants, peeled and cut
- 3 tablespoons of olive oil
- 2 onions, sliced
- 6 cloves of garlic, minced
- 2 teaspoons of oregano
- 1 cinnamon stick
- 1 teaspoon of salt
- 1 teaspoon of pepper
- 1 bay leaf
- 150g of dried chickpeas
- 3 tomatoes, chopped
- 10g of parsley

Method:

1.Preheat the oven to 400°F/200°C

2.Peel and cut the eggplants, cut the mushrooms and everything else that needs to be cut

3.Place on baking sheet and cook for 6 minutes

4.Then transfer to the slow cooker

5.Cook for four hours on high

6.Remove the cinnamon stick and the bay leaf

7.Serve and enjoy

Nutritional Information:

Calories: 219 kcal, Fats: 7 grams, Carbohydrates: 33 grams, Protein: 9 grams

Barley Soup

Ingredients:

- 1 tablespoon of olive oil

- 1 onion, diced

- 1 stalk of celery, diced

- 1 carrot, diced

- 2liter of water

- 1liter of vegetable broth

- 100g of pearl barley

- 40g of black beans

- 50g of great northern beans

- 50g of kidney beans

- 1 tablespoon of chili powder

- 1 teaspoon of cumin

- ½ teaspoon of oregano

- ¾ teaspoon of salt

Method:

1.Cut everything up that needs to be cut and mix it all together in the Dutch oven

2.Put on low heat and cook for about two and a half hours

3.Serve and enjoy

Nutritional Information:

Calories: 205 kcal, Fats: 3 grams, Carbohydrates: 35 grams, Protein: 11 grams

Squash Quinoa Casserole

Ingredients:

- 360g of tomatillos, de-husked and chopped

- 450g of cherry tomatoes, chopped

- 1 bell pepper, chopped

- 80g of chopped onion

- 1 tablespoon of lime juice

- 1 teaspoon of salt

- 170g of quinoa

- 110g of feta cheese

- 1kg of yellow squash, sliced

- 2 tablespoons of oregano

Method:

1.Chop everything up that needs to get cut

2.Place everything in the slow cooker and cook on low for four hours

3.Serve and enjoy

Nutritional Information:

Calories: 111 kcal, Fats: 3 grams, Carbohydrates: 18 grams, Protein: 5 grams

Pinto Bean Mix

Ingredients:

- 2 tablespoons of olive oil
- 2 carrots, sliced
- 1 onion, sliced
- 4 cloves of garlic, minced
- 3 tablespoons of chili powder
- 2 tablespoons of balsamic vinegar
- 200g of pinto beans
- 1 red bell pepper, diced
- 240g of tomato sauce
- 150ml of water
- 2 tablespoons of soy sauce
- 2 tablespoons of tomato paste
- 400g of green cabbage, sliced
- 1 zucchini, chopped
- 175g of corn
- 3 tablespoons of honey mustard
- 1 teaspoon of salt
- 10 whole wheat hamburger buns

Method:

1.Cut up everything that needs to get cut up and place in slow cooker

2.Cook on high heat for 5 hours with the other ingredients

3.Place the cabbage and the zucchini in the last 30 minutes

4.Serve on buns and enjoy

Nutritional Information:

Calories: 283 kcal, Fats: 6 grams, Carbohydrates: 51 grams, Protein: 11 grams

Mexican Spaghetti and Sauce

Ingredients:

- 150g of chopped onion
- 1 tablespoon of olive oil
- 900g of meatless spaghetti sauce
- 1 can/200g of black beans
- 200g of diced tomatoes
- 175g of corn
- 70g cup of salsa
- 120g of green chilies
- 1 tablespoon of chili powder
- ¼ teaspoon of pepper
- 1 box/130g of spaghetti

Method:

1.Chop the onion up and cook in a skillet with the oil until they are clear

2.In a large saucepan combine everything else together and stir well

3.Cook on a simmer for about 20 minutes

4.Serve sauce over spaghetti noodles and enjoy

Nutritional Information:

Calories: 216.3 kcal, Fats: 4.8 grams, Carbohydrates: 36.1 grams, Protein: 9.0 grams

Chicken Soup

Ingredients:

- 3-4 chicken breasts

- 8 cloves fresh garlic, chopped

- Low salt and freshly ground pepper, to taste

- 200g cabbage (thinly shredded)

- 1 green bell pepper (deseeded, diced)

- 1 yellow summer squash (diced)

- 2 zucchini squash, cut up

- 6 to 8 baby potatoes cut up

- 1x 120g can chopped green chillies

- 1 tsp sage

- 1 tsp each of: dried basil, oregano, and parsley

- 1x 420g can diced tomatoes

- 600ml chicken broth, as needed

- A dash or two of balsamic vinegar to taste

- Olive oil, as needed

Method:

1.Drizzle some olive oil into a slow cooker and lay the chicken breasts in it, with half the chopped garlic. Season a little with sea salt and pepper.

2.In a bowl, combine the bell pepper, shredded cabbage, zucchini squashes, potatoes, and green chilies, tossing them with another drizzle of olive oil. Season the mixture with sea salt, black pepper, herbs and toss to coat.

3.Pour the veggie mix into the slow cooker in an even layer. Add in the tomatoes, chicken broth, and a small dash of balsamic vinegar, to taste.

4.The liquid content should just about cover the veggies in the pot. If you like, you can add more broth to get better consistency of a soup.

5.Cover the pot and let it cook for up to 5 to 6 hours, or until the chicken is tender and easily breaks apart into pieces.

Nutritional Information:

Calories: 277 kcal; Fats: 8.9g; Carbohydrates: 13.6g; Protein: 35.0g

Slow Cooked Macaroni with Cheese

Ingredients:

- 2 eggs

- 400ml of milk

- 360g of evaporated milk

- 250g of elbow macaroni

- 400g of shredded cheddar cheese

- 1 teaspoon of salt

- ½ teaspoon of pepper

Method:
1.Combine everything into the slow cooker and stir well
2.Cook on low for about five hours and stir every so often

3.Serve and enjoy

Nutritional Information:

Calories: 592 kcal, Fats: 33.5 grams, Carbohydrates: 39.5 grams, Protein: 32.6 grams

Turkey Stew with Green Chilies

Ingredients:

- 240g butternut squash (peeled and diced)

- 500g ground turkey

- 1 large potatoe (optional & diced)

- 3 medium carrots (peeled and chopped)

- 1 onion (diced)

- 4 cloves garlic (minced)

- 1 tsp cumin

- 1 tsp chili powder

- 150g roasted chopped green chili

- 1liter chicken stock

- Low salt and black pepper to taste

For serving:

- Juice from 1 lime

- 2-3 tbsp chopped cilantro

- 1-2 tsp agave nectar, as needed

Method:

1.Firstly, brown the ground pork in a skillet and take out the excess fat, if any.

2.Now add the pork to the slow cooker with the remaining ingredients up to sea salt and black pepper. Stir well to combine.

3.Cover and cook until the pork is done.

4.About 20 minutes before serving, stir in the lime juice and cilantro. Add some sweetener, if needed, to balance out the spice and if you need a little more liquid, add more broth to it and heat through.

Nutritional information:

Calories: 423 kcal; Fats: 13.5g; Carbohydrates: 44.7g; Protein: 36.3g

Refried Beans

Ingredients:

- 1 onion, chopped

- 600g of pinto beans

- 50g of chopped jalapeno pepper

- 2 tablespoons of minced garlic

- 5 teaspoons of salt

- ¾ teaspoons of pepper

- 1/8 teaspoon of cumin

- 1700ml of water

Method:

1.Chop up the onion and place in the slow cooker with everything else

2.Cook on high for about five hours

3.Once the beans are cooked, strain them and mash them

4.Serve and enjoy

Nutritional Information:

Calories: 139 kcal, Fats: 0.5 grams, Carbohydrates: 25.4 grams, Protein: 8.5 grams

Vegetable and Cheese Soup

Ingredients:

- 730g of creamed corn
- 220g of potatoes, peeled and cubed
- 50g of carrots, chopped
- ½ onion, chopped
- 1 teaspoon of celery seed
- ½ teaspoon of pepper
- 1500ml of vegetable broth
- 600g of cheese sauce

Method:

1.Peel and chop everything then place in the slow cooker

2.Stir well and cook on medium heat for about five hours

3.Serve and enjoy

Nutritional Information:

Calories: 316 kcal, Fats: 16.5 grams, Carbohydrates: 32.1 grams, Protein: 11.9 grams

Vegetable and Black Bean Soup

Ingredients:

- 500g of black beans
- 1500ml of water
- 1 carrot, chopped
- 1 stalk of celery, chopped
- 1 red onion, chopped
- 6 cloves of garlic, crushed
- 2 green bell peppers, chopped
- 2 jalapeno peppers, chopped
- 50g of lentils
- 4 diced tomatoes
- 2 tablespoons of chili powder
- 2 teaspoons of ground cumin
- ½ teaspoon of oregano
- ½ teaspoon of pepper
- 1 tablespoon of salt
- 100g of white rice

Method:

1.Chop and mince everything and them mix it all together in the slow cooker

2.Place on high heat and cook for about three hours

3.Serve and enjoy

Nutritional Information:

Calories: 231 kcal, Fats: 1.2 grams, Carbohydrates: 43.4 grams, Protein: 12.6 grams

Pasta with Homemade Tomato Sauce

Ingredients:

- 10 plum tomatoes, peeled and crushed

- ½ of an onion, chopped

- 1 teaspoon of garlic, minced

- 60ml of olive oil

- 1 teaspoon of oregano

- 1 teaspoon of basil

- 1 teaspoon of cayenne pepper

- 1 teaspoon of salt

- 1 teaspoon of pepper

- 1 pinch of cinnamon

- 1 box/150g of bowtie pasta

Method:

1.Peel and crush the tomatoes, mince the garlic and chop the onion

2.Place everything in the slow cooker and stir well

3.Cook on high for about four hours or so

4.Serve and enjoy

Nutritional Information:

Calories: 105 kcal, Fats: 9.3 grams, Carbohydrates: 5.5 grams, Protein: 1.2 grams

Delicious Rice Casserole

Ingredients:

- 2 onions, chopped

- 3 stalks of celery, sliced

- 1kg of mixed rice

- 600ml of water

- 1 can/200ml of mushroom soup

- 130g of butter

- 230g of shredded American cheese

- 35g of mushrooms, sliced

Method:

1.Chop everything up that needs to get cut and place in the slow cooker

2.Add everything else but the cheese in the slow cooker

3.Cook on high for about four hours

4.Serve and enjoy with the shredded cheese on top

Nutritional Information:

Calories: 408 kcal, Fats: 23 grams, Carbohydrates: 39.5 grams, Protein: 11.6 grams

Potato Soup Slow Cooker Style

Ingredients:

- 1 onion, chopped

- 1liter of chicken broth

- 500ml of water

- 5 potatoes, diced

- ½ teaspoon of salt

- ½ teaspoon of dill weed

- ½ teaspoon of pepper

- 60g of all-purpose flour

- 400g of half and half cream

- 360ml of evaporated milk

Method:

1.Chop and dice everything that needs to get cut and combine all of the ingredients into the slow cooker

2.Cook on high heat for about three and a half hours

3.Serve and enjoy, try with some sour cream and some shredded cheese on top

Nutritional Information:

Calories: 553 kcal, Fats: 19.3 grams, Carbohydrates: 74.2 grams, Protein: 22 grams

Split Pea Soup

Ingredients:

- 500g of split peas
- 1 onion, chopped
- 3 carrots, chopped
- 3 stalks of celery, chopped
- 2 cloves of garlic, minced
- 1/8 teaspoon of pepper
- 1 pinch of red pepper flakes
- 2liter of chicken broth

Method:
1.Chop everything up that needs to get cut and place all of the ingredients into the slow cooker

2.Cook on high heat for about five hours, stirring every so often

3.Serve and enjoy

Nutritional Information:

Calories: 273 kcal, Fats: 3.4 grams, Carbohydrates: 44 grams, Protein: 17.7 grams

Onion Soup

Ingredients:

- 6 tablespoons of butter

- 4 onions, sliced

- 2 cloves of garlic, minced

- 130ml of cooking sherry

- 1700ml of vegetable broth

- 1 teaspoon of salt

- ¼ teaspoon of thyme

- 1 bay leaf

- 8 slices of French bread

- 50g of shredded parmesan cheese

- 40g of shredded Colby jack cheese

- 30g of cheddar cheese

- 2 tablespoons of mozzarella cheese

Method:

1.Chop everything up that needs to be cut and place in the slow cooker

2.Add in everything else but the cheese and the bread

3.Broil the bread in the oven for about three months

4.Place the slow cooker on high heat and cook for five hours

5.Serve and enjoy with some of the bread and the cheese on top

Nutritional Information:

Calories: 250 kcal, Fats: 14.7 grams, Carbohydrates: 17.5 grams, Protein: 11 grams

Zucchini Soup

Ingredients:

- 200g of chopped celery

- 1kg of zucchini, sliced

- 6 tomatoes, diced

- 2 green bell peppers, sliced

- 150g of chopped onion

- 2 teaspoons of salt

- 1 teaspoon of oregano

- 1 teaspoon of Italian seasoning

- 1 teaspoon of basil

- ¼ teaspoon of garlic powder

- 6 tablespoons of shredded parmesan cheese

Method:

1.Chop up everything that needs to get cut up and place in the slow cooker except for the cheese

2.Stir well and put on high heat

3.Cook for about three and a half hours

4.Serve and enjoy with some of the shredded cheese on top

Nutritional Information:

Calories: 389 kcal, Fats: 23.6 grams, Carbohydrates: 25.8 grams, Protein: 21.8 grams

Lentil Soup

Ingredients:

- 400g of brown lentils

- 750ml of chicken broth

- 1 bay leaf

- 50g of carrots, chopped

- 100g of celery, chopped

- 150g of onion, chopped

- 1 teaspoon of Worcestershire sauce

- ½ teaspoon of garlic powder

- ¼ teaspoon of nutmeg

- 5 drops of hot sauce

- ¼ teaspoon of caraway seed

- ½ teaspoon of celery salt

- 1 tablespoon of parsley

- ½ teaspoon of pepper

Method:

1.Cut up everything that needs to get cut up

2.Place in the slow cooker and cook on high for about five hours

3.Remove the bay leaf

4.Serve and enjoy

Nutritional Information:

Calories: 221 kcal, Fats: 2.3 grams, Carbohydrates: 34.2 grams, Protein: 16 grams

Taco Soup

Ingredients:

- 1 onion, chopped
- 1 can of chili beans
- 1 can of kidney beans
- 1 can of corn
- 1 can of tomato sauce
- 500ml of water
- 6 tomatoes, diced
- 2 green chili peppers
- 3 tablespoons of taco seasoning mix

Method:
1.Cut up everything that needs to be diced

2.Place in the slow cooker and stir well

3.Cook on high for about three and a half hours

4.Serve and enjoy, try with some sour cream and shredded cheese on top

Nutritional Information:

Calories: 362 kcal, Fats: 16.3 grams, Carbohydrates: 37.8 grams, Protein: 18.2 grams

Cabbage Soup

Ingredients:

- 2 tablespoons of vegetable oil
- 1 onion, chopped
- 500g of cabbage, chopped
- 2 cans/400g of red kidney beans
- 500ml of water
- 1200ml of tomato sauce
- 4 tablespoons of seasoned salt
- 1 ½ teaspoons of cumin
- 1 teaspoon of salt
- 1 teaspoon of pepper

Method:

1.Chop the cabbage and the onion up

2.Place in slow cooker with everything else

3.Cook on high for four hours

4.Serve and enjoy

Nutritional Information:

Calories: 211 kcal, Fats: 8.7 grams, Carbohydrates: 20.3 grams, Protein: 14.1 grams

Corn Chowder

Ingredients:

- 5 potatoes, peeled and cubed
- 2 onions, chopped
- 3 stalks of celery, chopped
- 1 can/200g of whole kernel corn
- 2 tablespoons of butter
- ½ teaspoon of salt
- ½ teaspoon of pepper
- 2 tablespoons of seasoned salt
- 1 can/200ml of evaporated milk

Method:

1.Peel and cube the potatoes

2.Chop the onions and the celery

3.Combine everything in the slow cooker

4.Set on high heat and cook for about four hours

5.Serve and enjoy

Nutritional Information:

Calories: 266 kcal, Fats: 8.8 grams, Carbohydrates: 37.8 grams, Protein: 11.2 grams

Tofu Curry

Ingredients:

- 500g tofu (firm; cubed)
- 350g sweet corn
- 450ml coconut milk
- 60g curry paste
- 500ml vegetable stock
- 180g tomato paste (canned)
- 1 yellow pepper (chopped)
- 1 red pepper (chopped)
- 1 sweet onion (chopped)
- 3 garlic cloves (minced)
- 2 ginger (minced)
- 1 tbsp garam masala
- 1 tsp low salt
- Cilantro (for garnishing)

Method:

1.Start by cutting the tofu into ½ inch/1.5cm cubes and add it to a large slow cooker.

2.Next add the chopped onion, peppers; ginger and garlic to the slow cooker as well followed by the corn, vegetable stock, tomato paste, coconut milk and spices.

3.Stir well! Then cover and allow the curry to cook on high heat for approximately 3 to 4 hours.

4.Serve over brown rice or as desired.

Nutritional Information:

Calories: 328 kcal, Fats: 7 grams, Carbohydrates: 53.8 grams, Protein: 12.8 grams

Oatmeal with Cherries

Ingredients:

- 1liter fat-free milk

- 1liter water

- 320g steel-cut oats

- 50g raisins

- 70g dried cherries

- 60g dried apricots, chopped

- 1 teaspoon molasses

- 1 teaspoon cinnamon (or pumpkin pie spice)

Method:

1.In a slow cooker combine all of the ingredients. Turn heat to low.

2.Put the lid on and cook overnight for 8 to 9 hours.

3.Spoon into bowls and serve.

Nutrition Information:

Calories: 240kcal, fat: 2.5 g; carbohydrates: 47 g; protein: 11 g protein

Sauerkraut soup

Ingredients:

- 1 can/250ml of mushroom soup
- 1 can/250ml of chicken soup
- 700ml of water
- 1liter of chicken broth
- 250g of sauerkraut
- 1 onion, diced
- 3 carrots, chopped
- 5 potatoes, peeled and diced
- 1 teaspoon of dill weed
- 1 teaspoon of garlic, minced
- ½ teaspoon of salt
- ½ teaspoon of pepper

Method:

1.Peel and dice the potatoes

2.Cut the carrots and the onions

3.Mince the garlic

4.Combine everything into the slow cooker

5.Put on high heat and cook for four hours

6.Serve and enjoy

Nutritional Information:

Calories: 387 kcal, Fats: 23.4 grams, Carbohydrates: 26.4 grams, Protein: 17.7 grams

Lima Bean Soup

Ingredients:

- 300g of lima beans

- 1 can/200g of butter beans

- 2 potatoes, diced

- 2 stalks of celery, chopped

- 2 onions, chopped

- 3 carrots, sliced

- 60g of butter

- ½ tablespoon of diced marjoram

- 1 teaspoon of salt

- ½ teaspoon of pepper

- 3 cans/750ml of vegetable broth

Method:

1.Dice and cut everything that needs to be cut up

2.Place in the slow cooker with everything else

3.Set on high for four hours

4.Serve and enjoy

Nutritional Information:

Calories: 326 kcal, Fats: 11.4 grams, Carbohydrates: 43.7 grams, Protein: 13 grams

Veggy Minestrone Soup

Ingredients:

- 1500ml of vegetable broth
- 4 tomatoes, diced
- 1 can/200g of kidney beans
- 1 onion, chopped
- 2 stalks of celery, chopped
- 150g of green beans
- 1 zucchini, chopped
- 3 cloves of garlic, minced
- 1 tablespoon of parsley
- 1 ½ teaspoons of oregano
- 1 teaspoon of salt
- ¾ teaspoon of thyme
- ¼ teaspoon of pepper
- 75g of elbow noodles
- 900g of spinach, chopped
- 25g of shredded parmesan cheese

Method:

1.Chop everything up that needs to get cut up

2.Place in the slow cooker with everything but the cheese

3.Put on high for four hours or so

4.Serve and enjoy with the cheese on top

Nutritional Information:

Calories: 138 kcal, Fats: 1.7 grams, Carbohydrates: 25.2 grams, Protein: 6.9 grams

Spicy Thai Soup

Ingredients:

- 1300ml of vegetable broth
- 250ml of white wine(optional)
- 250ml of water
- 1 yellow onion, chopped
- 3 green onions, chopped
- 4 carrots, chopped
- 4 stalks of celery, chopped
- ½ teaspoon of salt
- 1 teaspoon of pepper
- 1 tablespoon of curry powder
- ½ tablespoon of sage
- ½ teaspoon of seasoned salt
- ½ tablespoon of oregano
- 1 teaspoon of cayenne pepper
- 2 tablespoons of vegetable oil
- 1 chili pepper, seeded and chopped
- 1 box/130g of rice noodles

Method:

1.Chop everything up that needs to get cut up

2.Place in the slow cooker

3.Cook on high for around five hours or until everything is tender

4.Serve and enjoy

Nutritional Information:

Calories: 131, Fats: 3 grams, Carbohydrates: 14.5 grams, Protein: 7.9 grams

Lentil and Mushroom Stew

Ingredients:

- 2 quarts/1800ml of vegetable broth

- 150g of mushrooms, sliced

- 30g of shiitake mushrooms, chopped

- 150g of uncooked pearl barley

- 150 of lentils

- 15g of onion flakes

- 2 teaspoons of minced garlic

- 2 teaspoons of pepper

- 3 bay leaves

- 1 teaspoon of basil

- 1 teaspoon of salt

Method:
1.Cut up everything and place in slow cooker

2.Stir well and cook on high heat for four hours

3.Remove bay leaves

4.Serve and enjoy

Nutritional Information:

Calories: 213 kcal, Fats: 1.2 grams, Carbohydrates: 43.9 grams, Protein: 8.4 grams

Pumpkin Goulash

Ingredients:

- 6 diced tomatoes
- 1 tablespoon of brown sugar(optional)
- 2 tablespoons of olive oil
- 1 onion, chopped
- 1 teaspoon of ginger
- 1 teaspoon of cinnamon
- 1 teaspoon of cumin
- 1 tablespoon of coriander
- 1 can/200g of garbanzo beans
- 1,5kg of fresh pumpkin, peeled and cut into small chunks
- 1 teaspoon of salt
- 1 teaspoon of cornstarch
- 50ml of water

Method:

1.Peel and cut the pumpkin up

2.Chop up everything else that needs to get cut up

3.Place it all in the slow cooker

4.Cook on high heat for about four hours

5.Serve and enjoy

Nutritional Information:

Calories: 330 kcal, Fats: 7.9 grams, Carbohydrates: 37.2 grams, Protein: 28.4 grams

Image sources/Printing information

Pictures cover: depositphotos. com;

@ bhofack2; @ ca2hill; @ Juliedeshaies; @ robynmac

Print edition black and white paperback:

Amazon Media EU S.à.r.l.

5 Rue Plaetis

L-2338 Luxembourg

Other printouts:

epubli, a service of neopubli GmbH, Berlin

Publisher:

BookRix GmbH & Co. KG

Sonnenstraße 23

80331 München

Deutschland

Manufactured by Amazon.ca
Acheson, AB

11697731R00057